Bee Positive

A 52-Week Positivity Journal

Bee illustration by yabayee via Pixabay

Font: Architext via 1001fonts.com

ISBN: 9781678779832

www.jeniferjones.com

HOW TO USE THIS JOURNAL

Each day, write down three good things that happened. Use the pages at the end of each week to jot down more good things, or use them to note your dreams and goals, or sketch a doodle or two!

Honey, it's gonna be a great week

Good things that happened this week:

Monday

1.

2.

3.

Tuesday

1.

2.

3.

Wednesday

1.

2.

3.

Thursday

1.

2.

3.

Friday

1.

2.

3.

Saturday

1.

2.

3.

Sunday

1.

2.

3.

Notes

Notes

You're the queen bee

Good things that happened this week:

Monday

1.

2.

3.

Tuesday

1.

2.

3.

Wednesday

1.

2.

3.

Thursday

1.

2.

3.

Friday

1.

2.

3.

Saturday

1.

2.

3.

Sunday

1.

2.

3.

Notes

Notes

Buzz off, bad attitude

Good things that happened this week:

Monday

1.

2.

3.

Tuesday

1.

2.

3.

Wednesday

1.

2.

3.

Thursday

1.

2.

3.

Friday

1.

2.

3.

Saturday

1.

2.

3.

Sunday

1.

2.

3.

Notes

Notes

Sometimes you just have to wing it

Good things that happened this week:

Monday

1.

2.

3.

Tuesday

1.

2.

3.

Wednesday

1.

2.

3.

Thursday

1.

2.

3.

Friday

1.

2.

3.

Saturday

1.

2.

3.

Sunday

1.

2.

3.

Notes

Notes

Honey, you can do this

Good things that happened this week:

Monday

1.

2.

3.

Tuesday

1.

2.

3.

Wednesday

1.

2.

3.

Thursday

1.

2.

3.

Friday

1.

2.

3.

Saturday

1.

2.

3.

Sunday

1.

2.

3.

Notes

Notes

Fly through the week with happy thoughts

Good things that happened this week:

Monday

1.

2.

3.

Tuesday

1.

2.

3.

Wednesday

1.

2.

3.

Thursday

1.

2.

3.

Friday

1.

2.

3.

Saturday

1.

2.

3.

Sunday

1.

2.

3.

Notes

Notes

Don't forget to stop and smell the flowers

Good things that happened this week:

Monday

1.

2.

3.

Tuesday

1.

2.

3.

Wednesday

1.

2.

3.

Thursday

1.

2.

3.

Friday

1.

2.

3.

Saturday

1.

2.

3.

Sunday

1.

2.

3.

Notes

Notes

Bee on your best bee-havior

Good things that happened this week:

Monday

1.

2.

3.

Tuesday

1.

2.

3.

Wednesday

1.

2.

3.

Thursday

1.

2.

3.

Friday

1.

2.

3.

Saturday

1.

2.

3.

Sunday

1.

2.

3.

Notes

Notes

Hey bad attitude, mind your own beeswax

Good things that happened this week:

Monday

1.

2.

3.

Tuesday

1.

2.

3.

Wednesday

1.

2.

3.

Thursday

1.

2.

3.

Friday

1.

2.

3.

Saturday

1.

2.

3.

Sunday

1.

2.

3.

Notes

Notes

You're bee-utiful

Good things that happened this week:

Monday

1.

2.

3.

Tuesday

1.

2.

3.

Wednesday

1.

2.

3.

Thursday

1.

2.

3.

Friday

1.

2.

3.

Saturday

1.

2.

3.

Sunday

1.

2.

3.

Notes

Notes

Hive-five! You're doing great!

Good things that happened this week:

Monday

1.

2.

3.

Tuesday

1.

2.

3.

Wednesday

1.

2.

3.

Thursday

1.

2.

3.

Friday

1.

2.

3.

Saturday

1.

2.

3.

Sunday

1.

2.

3.

Notes

Notes

Honey, you've got this

Good things that happened this week:

Monday

1.

2.

3.

Tuesday

1.

2.

3.

Wednesday

1.

2.

3.

Thursday

1.

2.

3.

Friday

1.

2.

3.

Saturday

1.

2.

3.

Sunday

1.

2.

3.

Notes

Notes

Want to bee happy? Bee positive!

Good things that happened this week:

Monday

1.

2.

3.

Tuesday

1.

2.

3.

Wednesday

1.

2.

3.

Thursday

1.

2.

3.

Friday

1.

2.

3.

Saturday

1.

2.

3.

Sunday

1.

2.

3.

Notes

Notes

I'm buzzing with excitement for the week

Good things that happened this week:

Monday

1.

2.

3.

Tuesday

1.

2.

3.

Wednesday

1.

2.

3.

Thursday

1.

2.

3.

Friday

1.

2.

3.

Saturday

1.

2.

3.

Sunday

1.

2.

3.

Notes

Notes

This week is going to be sweet

Good things that happened this week:

Monday

1.

2.

3.

Tuesday

1.

2.

3.

Wednesday

1.

2.

3.

Thursday

1.

2.

3.

Friday

1.

2.

3.

Saturday

1.

2.

3.

Sunday

1.

2.

3.

Notes

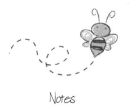

Notes

Don't bee buzzy all the time, bee sure and rest

Good things that happened this week:

Monday

1.

2.

3.

Tuesday

1.

2.

3.

Wednesday

1.

2.

3.

Thursday

1.

2.

3.

Friday

1.

2.

3.

Saturday

1.

2.

3.

Sunday

1.

2.

3.

Notes

Notes

Honey, it's gonna be a great week

Good things that happened this week:

Monday

1.

2.

3.

Tuesday

1.

2.

3.

Wednesday

1.

2.

3.

Thursday

1.

2.

3.

Friday

1.

2.

3.

Saturday

1.

2.

3.

Sunday

1.

2.

3

.

Notes

Notes

You're the queen bee

Good things that happened this week:

Monday

1.

2.

3.

Tuesday

1.

2.

3.

Wednesday

1.

2.

3.

Thursday

1.

2.

3.

Friday

1.

2.

3.

Saturday

1.

2.

3.

Sunday

1.

2.

3.

Notes

Notes

Buzz off, bad attitude

Good things that happened this week:

Monday

1.

2.

3.

Tuesday

1.

2.

3.

Wednesday

1.

2.

3.

Thursday

1.

2.

3.

Friday

1.

2.

3.

Saturday

1.

2.

3.

Sunday

1.

2.

3.

Notes

Notes

Sometimes you just have to wing it

Good things that happened this week:

Monday

1.

2.

3.

Tuesday

1.

2.

3.

Wednesday

1.

2.

3.

Thursday

1.

2.

3.

Friday

1.

2.

3.

Saturday

1.

2.

3.

Sunday

1.

2.

3.

Notes

Notes

Honey, you can do this

Good things that happened this week:

Monday

1.

2.

3.

Tuesday

1.

2.

3.

Wednesday

1.

2.

3.

Thursday

1.

2.

3.

Friday

1.

2.

3.

Saturday

1.

2.

3.

Sunday

1.

2.

3.

Notes

Notes

Fly through the week with happy thoughts

Good things that happened this week:

Monday

1.

2.

3.

Tuesday

1.

2.

3.

Wednesday

1.

2.

3.

Thursday

1.

2.

3.

Friday

1.

2.

3.

Saturday

1.

2.

3.

Sunday

1.

2.

3.

Notes

Notes

Don't forget to stop and smell the flowers

Good things that happened this week:

Monday

1.

2.

3.

Tuesday

1.

2.

3.

Wednesday

1.

2.

3.

Thursday

1.

2.

3.

Friday

1.

2.

3.

Saturday

1.

2.

3.

Sunday

1.

2.

3.

Notes

Notes

Bee on your best bee-havior

Good things that happened this week:

Monday

1.

2.

3.

Tuesday

1.

2.

3.

Wednesday

1.

2.

3.

Thursday

1.

2.

3.

Friday

1.

2.

3.

Saturday

1.

2.

3.

Sunday

1.

2.

3.

Notes

Notes

Hey bad attitude, mind your own beeswax

Good things that happened this week:

Monday

1.

2.

3.

Tuesday

1.

2.

3.

Wednesday

1.

2.

3.

Thursday

1.

2.

3.

Friday

1.

2.

3.

Saturday

1.

2.

3.

Sunday

1.

2.

3.

Notes

Notes

You're bee-utiful

Good things that happened this week:

Monday

1.

2.

3.

Tuesday

1.

2.

3.

Wednesday

1.

2.

3.

Thursday

1.

2.

3.

Friday

1.

2.

3.

Saturday

1.

2.

3.

Sunday

1.

2.

3.

Notes

Notes

Hive-five! You're doing great!

Good things that happened this week:

Monday

1.

2.

3.

Tuesday

1.

2.

3.

Wednesday

1.

2.

3.

Thursday

1.

2.

3.

Friday

1.

2.

3.

Saturday

1.

2.

3.

Sunday

1.

2.

3.

Notes

Notes

Honey, you've got this

Good things that happened this week:

Monday

1.

2.

3.

Tuesday

1.

2.

3.

Wednesday

1.

2.

3.

Thursday

1.

2.

3.

Friday

1.

2.

3.

Saturday

1.

2.

3.

Sunday

1.

2.

3.

Notes

Notes

Want to bee happy? Bee positive!

Good things that happened this week:

Monday

1.

2.

3.

Tuesday

1.

2.

3.

Wednesday

1.

2.

3.

Thursday

1.

2.

3.

Friday

1.

2.

3.

Saturday

1.

2.

3.

Sunday

1.

2.

3.

Notes

Notes

I'm buzzing with excitement for the week

Good things that happened this week:

Monday

1.

2.

3.

Tuesday

1.

2.

3.

Wednesday

1.

2.

3.

Thursday

1.

2.

3.

Friday

1.

2.

3.

Saturday

1.

2.

3.

Sunday

1.

2.

3.

Notes

Notes

This week is going to be sweet

Good things that happened this week:

Monday

1.

2.

3.

Tuesday

1.

2.

3.

Wednesday

1.

2.

3.

Thursday

1.

2.

3.

Friday

1.

2.

3.

Saturday

1.

2.

3.

Sunday

1.

2.

3.

Notes

Notes

Don't bee buzzy all the time, bee sure and rest

Good things that happened this week:

Monday

1.

2.

3.

Tuesday

1.

2.

3.

Wednesday

1.

2.

3.

Thursday

1.

2.

3.

Friday

1.

2.

3.

Saturday

1.

2.

3.

Sunday

1.

2.

3.

Notes

Notes

Honey, it's gonna be a great week

Good things that happened this week:

Monday

1.

2.

3.

Tuesday

1.

2.

3.

Wednesday

1.

2.

3.

Thursday

1.

2.

3.

Friday

1.

2.

3.

Saturday

1.

2.

3.

Sunday

1.

2.

3.

Notes

Notes

You're the queen bee

Good things that happened this week:

Monday

1.

2.

3.

Tuesday

1.

2.

3.

Wednesday

1.

2.

3.

Thursday

1.

2.

3.

Friday

1.

2.

3.

Saturday

1.

2.

3.

Sunday

1.

2.

3.

Notes

Notes

Buzz off, bad attitude

Good things that happened this week:

Monday

1.

2.

3.

Tuesday

1.

2.

3.

Wednesday

1.

2.

3.

Thursday

1.

2.

3.

Friday

1.

2.

3.

Saturday

1.

2.

3.

Sunday

1.

2.

3.

Notes

Notes

Sometimes you just have to wing it

Good things that happened this week:

Monday

1.

2.

3.

Tuesday

1.

2.

3.

Wednesday

1.

2.

3.

Thursday

1.

2.

3.

Friday

1.

2.

3.

Saturday

1.

2.

3.

Sunday

1.

2.

3.

Notes

Notes

Honey, you can do this

Good things that happened this week:

Monday

1.

2.

3.

Tuesday

1.

2.

3.

Wednesday

1.

2.

3.

Thursday

1.

2.

3.

Friday

1.

2.

3.

Saturday

1.

2.

3.

Sunday

1.

2.

3.

Notes

Notes

Fly through the week with happy thoughts

Good things that happened this week:

Monday

1.

2.

3.

Tuesday

1.

2.

3.

Wednesday

1.

2.

3.

Thursday

1.

2.

3.

Friday

1.

2.

3.

Saturday

1.

2.

3.

Sunday

1.

2

3.

Notes

Notes

Don't forget to stop and smell the flowers

Good things that happened this week:

Monday

1.

2.

3.

Tuesday

1.

2.

3.

Wednesday

1.

2.

3.

Thursday

1.

2.

3.

Friday

1.

2.

3.

Saturday

1.

2.

3.

Sunday

1.

2.

3.

Notes

Notes

Bee on your best bee-havior

Good things that happened this week:

Monday

1.

2.

3.

Tuesday

1.

2.

3.

Wednesday

1.

2.

3.

Thursday

1.

2.

3.

Friday

1.

2.

3.

Saturday

1.

2.

3.

Sunday

1.

2.

3.

Notes

Notes

Hey bad attitude, mind your own beeswax

Good things that happened this week:

Monday

1.

2.

3.

Tuesday

1.

2.

3.

Wednesday

1.

2.

3.

Thursday

1.

2.

3.

Friday

1.

2.

3.

Saturday

1.

2.

3.

Sunday

1.

2.

3.

Notes

Notes

You're bee-utiful

Good things that happened this week:

Monday

1.

2.

3.

Tuesday

1.

2.

3.

Wednesday

1.

2.

3.

Thursday

1.

2.

3.

Friday

1.

2.

3.

Saturday

1.

2.

3.

Sunday

1.

2.

3.

Notes

Notes

Hive-five! You're doing great!

Good things that happened this week:

Monday

1.

2.

3.

Tuesday

1.

2.

3.

Wednesday

1.

2.

3.

Thursday

1.

2.

3.

Friday

1.

2.

3.

Saturday

1.

2.

3.

Sunday

1.

2.

3.

Notes

Notes

Honey, you've got this

Good things that happened this week:

Monday

1.

2.

3.

Tuesday

1.

2.

3.

Wednesday

1.

2.

3.

Thursday

1.

2.

3.

Friday

1.

2.

3.

Saturday

1.

2.

3.

Sunday

1.

2.

3.

Notes

Notes

Want to bee happy? Bee positive!

Good things that happened this week:

Monday

1.

2.

3.

Tuesday

1.

2.

3.

Wednesday

1.

2.

3.

Thursday

1.

2.

3.

Friday

1.

2.

3.

Saturday

1.

2.

3.

Sunday

1.

2.

3.

Notes

Notes

I'm buzzing with excitement for the week

Good things that happened this week:

Monday

1.

2.

3.

Tuesday

1.

2.

3.

Wednesday

1.

2.

3.

Thursday

1.

2.

3.

Friday

1.

2.

3.

Saturday

1.

2.

3.

Sunday

1.

2.

3.

Notes

Notes

This week is going to be sweet

Good things that happened this week:

Monday

1.

2.

3.

Tuesday

1.

2.

3.

Wednesday

1.

2.

3.

Thursday

1.

2.

3.

Friday

1.

2.

3.

Saturday

1.

2.

3.

Sunday

1.

2.

3.

Notes

Notes

Don't bee buzzy all the time, bee sure and rest

Good things that happened this week:

Monday

1.

2.

3.

Tuesday

1.

2.

3.

Wednesday

1.

2.

3.

Thursday

1.

2.

3.

Friday

1.

2.

3.

Saturday

1.

2.

3.

Sunday

1.

2.

3.

Notes

Notes

Honey, it's gonna be a great week

Good things that happened this week:

Monday

1.

2.

3.

Tuesday

1.

2.

3.

Wednesday

1.

2.

3.

Thursday

1.

2.

3.

Friday

1.

2.

3.

Saturday

1.

2.

3.

Sunday

1.

2.

3.

Notes

Notes

You're the queen bee

Good things that happened this week:

Monday

1.

2.

3.

Tuesday

1.

2.

3.

Wednesday

1.

2.

3.

Thursday

1.

2.

3.

Friday

1.

2.

3.

Saturday

1.

2.

3.

Sunday

1.

2.

3.

Notes

Notes

Buzz off, bad attitude

Good things that happened this week:

Monday

1.

2.

3.

Tuesday

1.

2.

3.

Wednesday

1.

2.

3.

Thursday

1.

2.

3.

Friday

1.

2.

3.

Saturday

1.

2.

3.

Sunday

1.

2.

3.

Notes

Notes

Sometimes you just have to wing it

Good things that happened this week:

Monday

1.

2.

3.

Tuesday

1.

2.

3.

Wednesday

1.

2.

3.

Thursday

1.

2.

3.

Friday

1.

2.

3.

Saturday

1.

2.

3.

Sunday

1.

2.

3.

Notes

Notes

ABOUT THE AUTHOR

Jenifer Jones is the author of a book of poetry entitled *Truly Beloved: Reflections on Identity*.
Find her on Facebook and Instagram @jeniferjonespoems
Or on her website, www.jeniferjones.com

Made in the USA
Columbia, SC
19 December 2022

74574057R00129